DELIVERANCE

Of The Head

Vol. 1

GLORIA EHIEM

DELIVERANCE

Of The Head

Vol. 1

GLORIA EHIEM

Unless otherwise identified, Scripture quotations are taken from the Holy Bible.

Global Empowering Center Int'l
(a.k.a Mountain of the Lord)
Global Headquarters
Nottingham.

Printed in the United Kingdom
ISBN: 978-0-244-01712-5

www.global-empowering center.org.uk
www.mountainofthelord.org.uk
For Orders: globalempoweringcenter@yahoo.com
Phone: +44 7835121745

Introduction

In this book, you will access Divinely inspired Personal Deliverance Declarations and Prophesies that is aimed to help you gain total freedom and Victory Over any form of Negative Impartations, Implantations, Laying on of hands & Dedications you might have consciously or unconsciously being involved with either in your early years or as an adult.

I pray that as you declare these Prayers and Prophesies over yourself, every longstanding unfavorable patterns and stronghold shall be broken and you will encounter God power that is able to, change your circumstance and release you into your place and position of manifestation and exploits, in Jesus name amen.

Dedication

This book is dedicated to God, the Founder and General Overseer of Mountain of the Lord Intl' (a.k.a. Global Empowering Center);

To my Son Treasure, through whom God has taught me hope beyond measure, faith without limit, and joy beyond bound. I pray that you shall continually be a shining star in your generation as God has declared, and an instrument of tremendous blessing in the lives of many.

And to all who need a Supernatural revolution and a touch from God. It is my hope, desire, and prayer that this book would be the bold step you have sought for that is able to, change your circumstance forever.

How To Use This Book

Below are some ideas to guide you.

I. In other to effect spontaneous results; It is recommended to accompany these deliverance prayers with a Fast.

2. God's word is powerful, effective and sure, regardless of the means through which it was given. When using these prayers apply faith, knowing that God has already granted your request.

3. Personalize these declarations by including your name. You can retain the precise wording or change it to suit your own situation. And repeat it for as long as you are led.

4. Try using the present tense – it adds power to a personal declaration.

5. Always use the Bible verse associated with each declaration; Memorize the bible verses or write it out and use it to back up your declarations.

Finally, you can choose to use bold declarations in times of warfare or when breakthrough is needed. However, we do not always need to speak loudly in order for a declaration to be effective. The Hebrew word 'to meditate' also means 'to mutter'—to speak aloud to oneself—and this can even be done under our breath or quietly.

DELIVERANCE

Of The Head

Vol. 1

PSALM 27:6

SCRIPTURAL GUIDE

DELIVERANCE DECLARATION - DAY 1

Today - I declare that every negative deliberation and counsel assigned to keep my head down is intercepted and canceled by the power of the Holy Spirit; MY HEAD will henceforth be lifted up above my adversaries in Jesus name amen.

Note: Place your right hand on your head, as you Declare these Prophetic Prayers and the Scriptural guide for about 10 minutes.

ISAIAH 61:10

SCRIPTURAL GUIDE

DELIVERANCE DECLARATION - DAY 2

Today - I declare that the Hands of God has taken away every covering hindering my identity and preventing favor; And has bestowed on my head the oil of Joy and a crown of honor in Jesus name amen.

Note: Place your right hand on your head, as you Declare these Prophetic Prayers and the Scriptural guide for about 10 minutes.

GENESIS 7:17

SCRIPTURAL GUIDE

DELIVERANCE DECLARATION - DAY 3

Today - I declare that as the flood waters in Gen. 7:17, lifting the ark so that it rose above the surface of the earth; so shall my head be lifted far above life situations and circumstances, in Jesus name amen.

Note: Place your right hand on your head, as you Declare these Prophetic Prayers and the Scriptural guide over your head for about 10 minutes.

COLOSSIANS 2:14

SCRIPTURAL GUIDE

DELIVERANCE DECLARATION - DAY 4

Today - I declare that the blood of Jesus has set my head free and blotted out the handwriting of ordinances that was transferred into my life through the wrong laying on of hands in Jesus name amen.

Note: Place your right hand on your head, as you Declare these Prophetic Prayers and the Scriptural guide over your head for about 10 minutes.

JEREMIAH 29:11

SCRIPTURAL GUIDE

DELIVERANCE DECLARATION - DAY 5

Today - I declare that every carefully orchestrated imagination and thought assigned to alter my walk with God in this season is terminated by the power of the Holy Spirit in Jesus name amen.

Note: Place your right hand on your head, as you Declare these Prophetic Prayers and the Scriptural guide over your head for about 10 minutes.

PSALM 92:10

SCRIPTURAL GUIDE

DELIVERANCE DECLARATION - DAY 6

Today - I declare that God has exalted my head with the oil of prosperity, gladness, and favor; Henceforth every step I take begins to unlock doors of immeasurable blessings in Jesus name amen.

Note: Place your right hand on your head, as you Declare these Prophetic Prayers and the Scriptural guide over your head for about 10 minutes.

NUMBERS 23:23

SCRIPTURAL GUIDE

DELIVERANCE DECLARATION - DAY 7

Today - I declare that every manipulation targeted against the four lobes of my cerebrum: including the frontal, parietal, temporal, and occipital are permanently halted and terminated by the power of God in Jesus name amen.

Note: Place your right hand on your head, as you Declare these Prophetic Prayers and the Scriptural guide over your head for about 10 minutes.

GALATIANS 3:13

SCRIPTURAL GUIDE

DELIVERANCE DECLARATION - DAY 8

Today - I declare that every curse issued against my head cannot stand because the blood of Jesus has liberated me from all forms of curses, and ushered me into a new covenant of blessings in Jesus name amen.

Note: Place your right hand on your head, as you Declare these Prophetic Prayers and the Scriptural guide over your head for about 10 minutes.

2 TIMOTHY 1:7

SCRIPTURAL GUIDE

DELIVERANCE DECLARATION - DAY 9

Today - I declare that every seed of fear, uncertainty, anxiety, reproach, and failure sown into my memory by wrong voices and counsels; is crushed by the power of the Holy Spirit in Jesus name amen.

Note: Place your right hand on your head, as you Declare these Prophetic Prayers and the Scriptural guide over your head for about 10 minutes.

PSALM 51:7

SCRIPTURAL GUIDE

DELIVERANCE DECLARATION - DAY 10

Today - I declare that every character of my life that has consistently interfered with my breakthroughs is permanently terminated by the power of the Holy Spirit in Jesus name amen.

Note: Place your right hand on your head, as you Declare these Prophetic Prayers and the Scriptural guide over your head for about 10 minutes.

ACTS 1:8

SCRIPTURAL GUIDE

DELIVERANCE DECLARATION - DAY 11

Today - I declare that God has transformed my words, communication, expressions, and vocabularies by His Holy Spirit into the language of Power and Authority in Jesus name amen.

Note: Place your right hand on your head, as you Declare these Prophetic Prayers and the Scriptural guide over your head for about 10 minutes.

ISAIAH 53:5

SCRIPTURAL GUIDE

DELIVERANCE DECLARATION - DAY 12

Today - I declare that every hidden infirmity in my body (from the crown of my head to the sole of my feet) receives the fire of the Holy Spirit and dries up instantly in Jesus name amen.

Note: Place your right hand on your head, as you Declare these Prophetic Prayers and the Scriptural guide over your head for about 10 minutes.

2 CORINTHIANS 10:5

SCRIPTURAL GUIDE

DELIVERANCE DECLARATION - DAY 13

Today - I declare that every spiritual arrow fired into my head, in other to corrupt and destabilize my thoughts process is crushed and consumed by the fire of the Holy Spirit in Jesus name amen.

Note: Place your right hand on your head, as you Declare these Prophetic Prayers and the Scriptural guide over your head for about 10 minutes.

DEUTERONOMY 20:4

SCRIPTURAL GUIDE

DELIVERANCE DECLARATION - DAY 14

Today - I declare that any virtue sabotaged, diverted or stolen as a result of the wrong laying on of hands; is restored by the power of the Holy Spirit; Henceforth I will not miss the valuable contacts and opportunities due for me in Jesus name amen.

Note: Place your right hand on your head, as you Declare these Prophetic Prayers and the Scriptural guide over your head for about 10 minutes.

GALATIANS 6:17

SCRIPTURAL GUIDE

DELIVERANCE DECLARATION - DAY 15

Today - I declare that the influences of negative dedications in my life and destiny is canceled;
and any demonically projected marks associated with such influence are canceled by the blood of Jesus in Jesus name amen.

Note: Place your right hand on your head, as you Declare these Prophetic Prayers and the Scriptural guide over your head for about 10 minutes.

GALATIANS 6:17

SCRIPTURAL GUIDE

DELIVERANCE DECLARATION - DAY 16

Today - I declare that every contrary spirit, weakness, and addictions introduced into my life, due to the wrong ordination, dedication and laying on of hand is permanently erased out of my life by the blood of Jesus, in Jesus name amen.

Note: Place your right hand on your head, as you Declare these Prophetic Prayers and the Scriptural guide over your head for about 10 minutes.

ROMANS 6:14

SCRIPTURAL GUIDE

DELIVERANCE DECLARATION - DAY 17

Today - I declare that my head is liberated and delivered from strange battles, strange characters, strange occurrences, and patterns introduced through negative impartations and dedications in Jesus name amen.

Note: Place your right hand on your head, as you Declare these Prophetic Prayers and the Scriptural guide over your head for about 10 minutes.

PSALM 32:7

SCRIPTURAL GUIDE

DELIVERANCE DECLARATION - DAY 18

Today - I declare that my head receives a fresh anointing to retain revelations, valuable ideas, contacts and contents for consistent success and every hand that wants to rise as an opposition against this; withers by the consuming fire of God in Jesus name amen.

Note: Place your right hand on your head, as you Declare these Prophetic Prayers and the Scriptural guide over your head for about 10 minutes.

PSALM 18:35

SCRIPTURAL GUIDE

DELIVERANCE DECLARATION - DAY 19

Today - I declare total victory over every ministerial, educational, financial, emotional, marital etc struggles introduced into my life through negative implantations, impartations, and dedications in Jesus name amen.

Note: Place your right hand on your head, as you Declare these Prophetic Prayers and the Scriptural guide over your head for about 10 minutes.

GENESIS 50:20

SCRIPTURAL GUIDE

DELIVERANCE DECLARATION - DAY 20

Today - I declare that any emotional or psychological struggle introduced into my life as a result of wrong laying on of hands is terminated by the power of God in Jesus name amen.

Note: Place your right hand on your head, as you Declare these Prophetic Prayers and the Scriptural guide over your head for about 10 minutes.

ROMANS 8:28

SCRIPTURAL GUIDE

DELIVERANCE DECLARATION - DAY 21

Today - I declare that every occultic hand seeking to quench the fire of God in my life and manipulate my destiny receives the fire of God and withers in Jesus name amen.

Note: Place your right hand on your head, as you Declare these Prophetic Prayers and the Scriptural guide over your head for about 10 minutes.

THE END

NEED DEDICATED PRAYER PARTNERS?

We meet every Saturday Evening @ 7:10 pm Prompt on the Prophetic Prayer Mountain Where our Intercessors and the Prophetic team will minister to your individual need.

To Join
Dial Toll-Free No: 03309981261
Access Code: 301993

or Download
(freeconferencecall.com apps)
from android store or Iphone store Free

or Visit website
www.global-empowering-center.org
Click: Join Prayer Mountain

Please use Meeting ID:
propheticprayermountain

I AM NOT A CHRISTIAN OR I HAVE BACKSLIDED. HOW CAN I BENEFIT FROM YOUR MINISTRY?

In Revelation 3:20, Jesus said,...
"Behold, I stand at the door, and knock: if any man hear my voice, and open the door, I will come in to him, and will sup with him, and he with me".

It takes only "**2 minutes**" to make amends and begin to benefit from the endless blessings that comes with having a personal relationship with God.

SAY THIS PRAYER .....

"Father, I know that I have broken your laws and my sins have separated me from you. I am truly sorry, and now I want to turn away from my past sinful life toward you. Please forgive me, and help me avoid sinning again. I believe that your son, Jesus Christ died for my sins, was resurrected from the dead, is alive, and hears my prayer. I invite Jesus to become the Lord of my life, to rule and reign in my heart from this day forward. Please send your Holy Spirit to help me obey You, and to do Your will for the rest of my life. In Jesus' name I pray, Amen."

Other Books

I-Declare, is a daily Prophetic Declaration & Prayer Guide, Specially prepared under God's Divine Inspiration and Guidance to Equip you to Shift Atmospheres & Live SUPERNATURALLY daily.

ORDER FROM AMAZON.CO.UK OR GLOBAL-EMPOWERING-CENTER.ORG

Top Customer Reviews

A great resource

By SGS on 30 Nov. 2016

Verified Purchase

Spoken Word is powerful to change any situation. A great resource. I would most definitely would recommend this book to other

Comment Was this review helpful to you? Yes No Report abuse

1

4.0 out of 5 stars

Book Publication Enquiries;

www.global-empowering-center.org

Email: globalempoweringcenter@yahoo.com

Call: 07407810110

www.ingramcontent.com/pod-product-compliance
Ingram Content Group UK Ltd.
Pitfield, Milton Keynes, MK11 3LW, UK
UKHW020227250726
13967UKWH00001B/231